Dads

John Coy   photographs by Wing Young Huie

Carolrhoda Books

Minneapolis

Dads get up early

to start their day.

They fix.

They build.

They cook

and clean.

Dads share.

They teach.

They laugh and play.

Dads worry.

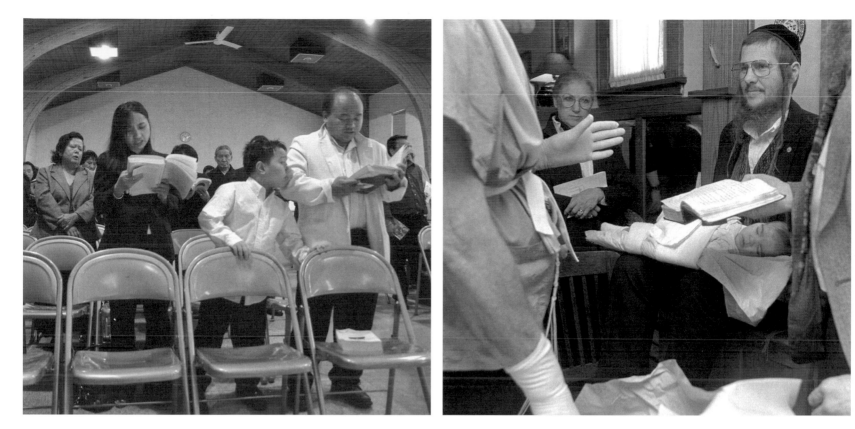

They pray.

They get frustrated.

They hug.

Dads correct.

They remember.

They wait.

They listen.

Dads help.

They protect.

They read. They sing.

Dads work hard and then they rest.

All through the day,

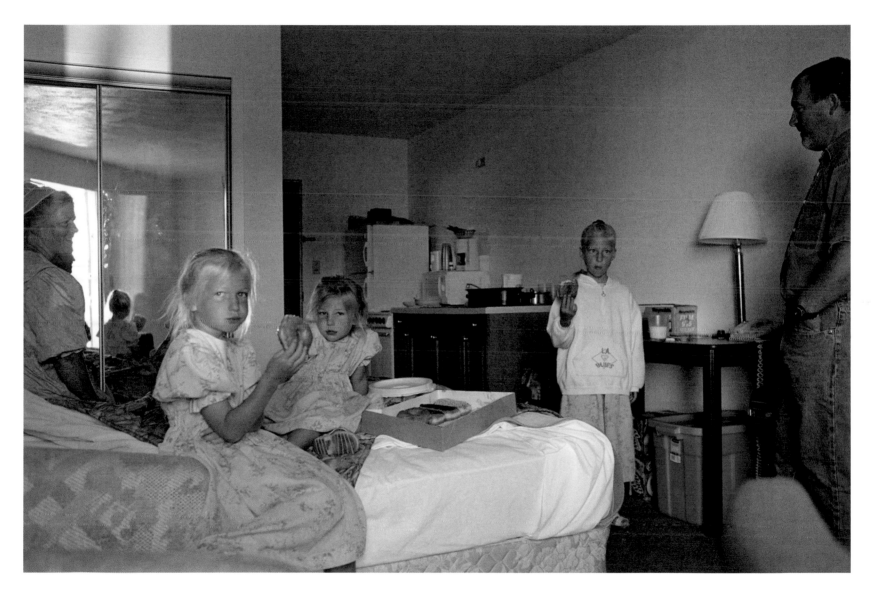

in so many ways.

Dads love.

John Coy

I am a writer because of being a father. When my daughter Sophia was little, I stayed home with her and we read tons of picture books. Reading to her was what inspired me to start writing my own stories. Now, she is the mother of twin boys and her husband John Moret stays home with them during the day. I am so impressed by all he does with them, including reading plenty of books.

Being a dad is the best job I've ever had, and I am struck by how much fatherhood has changed since I was a boy. I am pleased to see how engaged so many young fathers are with their children and the variety of activities they do together. *Dads* celebrates this engagement, acknowledging all that fathers are, and the ways being a dad continues to change.

I am grateful to Wing Young Huie, Carol Hinz, and Danielle Carnito for another memorable collaboration.

Wing Young Huie

For this book, I combed through my archive spanning forty years of my career, searching for photos of fathers and father figures. The earliest photo (page 12) is of my father sitting in the kitchen of our house in Duluth, Minnesota. That portrait, published in a local magazine, launched my career. In my hometown he was famous because he owned a successful Chinese restaurant, but to me he was a bit of a stranger because he worked all the time.

Scrutinizing him through the camera lens and following him around for a week was the most intimate experience I ever had with my dad. I have since photographed thousands of strangers I've met in all kinds of ways, often on the street. I try not to pre-visualize and instead just react to what I see. Hopefully my photos reflect the complexities and ambiguities of life—loaded with suggestion yet open-ended in what they suggest.

Publisher's Note

Adam Lerner

In 1959, Harry Lerner, my dad, founded a publishing company. I grew up surrounded by books, and I now have the great pleasure of publishing books for children—as well as being the father of two young men. Wing Young Huie photographed me together with my sons on a cold day early in 2019. He put us at ease as we sat together in a small library inside the Lerner Publishing Group offices. Every father has a unique relationship with his children, yet we also have much in common, wherever we are from and whatever our circumstances. I am so proud to have my family included among all those whose lives Wing has captured in his amazing body of work.

Carolrhoda Books®
An imprint of Lerner Publishing Group, Inc.
241 First Avenue North
Minneapolis, MN 55401 USA

For reading levels and more information, look up this title at www.lernerbooks.com.

Main body text set in ITC Avant Garde Gothic Standard.
Typeface provided by Adobe Systems.

Library of Congress Cataloging-in-Publication Data

The Cataloging-in-Publication Data for *Dads* is on file at the Library of Congress.
ISBN 978-1-5415-7839-5 (lib. bdg.)
ISBN 978-1-5415-8226-2 (eb pdf)

Manufactured in the United States of America
1-46937-47814-9/6/2019